SHADOW IN THE CLOUDS

The Story of Airships

Douglas Botting

Illustrated by Michael Jackson

Explorer 16   **Puffin Books**

Acknowledgements. The publishers and author would like to thank the following for their kind permission to reproduce the photographs appearing in this book:

Associated Press Ltd: p. 40; Beringer und Pampaluchi: title page; Deutsches Museum: p. 28; Charles Dollfus: p. 23; William Heinemann Ltd and Wilbur Cross for photographs from *Ghost Ship of the Pole* appearing on pp. 19, 21 and 23; Illustrated London News: pp. 35 and 36; Captain George Meager: p. 31; Radio Times Hulton Picture Library: pp. 4 and 11; The Royal Aeronautical Society: p. 15; Ullstein GmbH: p. 10; Zeppelin-Metallwerke GmbH: pp. 9 and 28.

Puffin Books: a Division of Penguin Books Ltd,
Harmondsworth, Middlesex, England
Penguin Books Inc., 7110 Ambassador Road, Baltimore, Maryland 21207, U.S.A.
Penguin Books Australia Ltd, Ringwood, Victoria, Australia
Penguin Books Canada Ltd, 41 Steelcase Road West, Markham, Ontario, Canada
Penguin Books (N.Z.) Ltd, 182–190 Wairau Road, Auckland 10, New Zealand

First published 1975

Text Copyright © 1975 by Douglas Botting
Colour Illustrations Copyright © 1975 by Michael Jackson

Made and printed in Great Britain by
Westerham Press Ltd, Westerham, Kent
Set in Monophoto Ehrhardt

(Title page) *The* Graf Zeppelin *returning home over the Swiss Alps after her Near East cruise in the spring of 1929.*

1 Ever since earliest times man has longed to take to the air and soar towards the sun like a god. But it wasn't until the end of the eighteenth century that he finally rose into the skies in the world's first successful aircraft, the balloon – the first step in man's long and hazardous climb towards mastery of the air.

Simply to float in the air wasn't enough, though. Almost at once the early aeronauts experienced the limitations of balloons. You couldn't steer them. They went where the wind took you. And all too often it took you where you didn't want to go.

'The vehicle, sir,' pronounced Dr Johnson, 'can serve no use until we can guide them. I had rather now find a medicine that can cure an asthma.' S 1973744

The balloon wasn't the perfect answer. It needed power to propel it and a rudder to steer it. If ships of the sea had sails, why shouldn't ships of the air have them too? And oars? And paddles? Why not flap wings like a bird? As each new invention failed the aeronauts tried something else. They tried man-power to drive paddle-wheels. They tried clockwork to drive airscrews. They even tried primitive rocket-power. Nothing worked. Nothing would budge the balloon from its obstinate course.

Then, in 1852, a French engineer called Henri Giffard tried steam. He didn't seem worried by the sparks that flew up from his boiler towards the inflammable gas above him, he just coaxed his craft forward in the direction he wanted to go. This was the first powered flight in history. Steam still wasn't the real answer – it was too heavy, too feeble – but it was a long time before anyone did any better.

At last, in 1884, two French Army engineers, Renard and Krebs, achieved truly dirigible – guided – flight. In an elongated balloon of Chinese silk and bamboo trellis-work they took off from Paris and under the power of their electric motor they flew in a wide circle and returned to the place from which they had started. Exactly one hundred years after the first balloon flight, the first airship was born.

But man was still not master of the air. Steam engines, gas engines and electric motors all suffered from the same defect – they had a poor power/weight ratio, the more powerful you made them, the heavier and less effective they became. As for the new Daimler petrol engine, it still seemed too primitive and unreliable. In 1897 it blew up a German aeronaut called Wolfaert in mid-air, and for a while this put a lot of aeronauts off altogether.

All the basics of airship design – the streamlined envelope, keel, rudder, elevators, ballonets, propeller, trim – had been worked out years ago. What was really needed was a light and powerful motor – and a man of genius to put the whole lot together and pioneer the navigation of the air.

In 1897, the year that Wolfaert was killed, that man arrived in Paris. His name was Alberto Santos-Dumont. Within a few years a new air age had begun.

Alberto Santos-Dumont shakes hands with a well-wisher before setting off on a flight over Paris in his 1901 prize-winning airship No. 6.

Alberto Santos-Dumont, the world's first truly successful airman, was born in Brazil in 1873 and brought up on his father's plantation in the rich coffee state of São Paulo. He was a small, shy, dreamy boy, already fascinated by manned flight. Lying on the veranda of his parents' house through the hot Brazilian afternoons he would gaze into the tropical sky where the birds soared and the clouds scudded and dream of exploring that aerial ocean in his own flying-machine. In 1953, he used to say, man would be master of the skies.

Such fantasies were considered very odd in the Brazilian society of his day. But Santos-Dumont was different from most other dreamers. In the first place, he was a very good engineer. In the second place, he was very rich. He didn't have to waste his time and talent earning a living.

In 1897 he took his first big step and left Brazil for Paris. He was determined to learn to fly and there was no better place than Paris to turn his dreams into reality. His first ascent into the sky in a hired gas balloon was a revelation. High above the clouds he lunched on roast beef, ice cream and champagne, while the sounds of church bells and dog barks came up from the invisible earth below, snowflakes fell into his champagne glass, and rainbows played around the balloon basket.

Santos-Dumont was so entranced that he ordered his own balloon – a minute bubble of silk that could be carried around in his valise – and in this he began to explore the lower regions of the air and learn about weather and air masses, winds and vertical currents and the effects of flying over different kinds of land or water. Unlike some of his rivals, he knew that he ought to get a thorough grounding as the pilot of a free balloon before going on to try to become the pilot of a powered airship.

It required courage to launch oneself into the sky in a machine nobody knew how to fly. It required confidence not to be discouraged by the experts who said it couldn't be done. In spite of all the dangers and all the scoffers, Santos-Dumont went ahead and built his airship *Santos-Dumont No. 1* in a little machine-shop not far from his flat in Paris. And it was at this point that he made the vital breakthrough in airship development. He had taken to driving around Paris in a little motor tricycle fitted with

Santos-Dumont lands his airship in the street outside his Paris flat and pops in for a cup of coffee.

one of the most compact and advanced petrol engines of that time. Why not, he argued, drive his new dirigible balloon with the same kind of engine that drove his motor tricycle? So he did, and it worked. The power/weight ratio problem had been solved.

Airship No. 1 was very small, but in September 1898 it actually managed to do a figure of eight in the air before it turned from the shape of a sausage into the shape of a banana and crashed. Santos-Dumont was ecstatic. He had navigated the air. He had experienced the utterly strange sensation of travel in an extra dimension – a curious combination of both horizontal and vertical movements. So Santos-Dumont built *Airship No. 2* and when that turned into a banana as well he built *Airship No. 3*.

No. 3 was three times bigger than *No. 1* and shaped more like a haggis or a melon. In November 1899, with only a few weeks of the nineteenth century to go, Santos-Dumont filled it with gas-lamp gas and took off. This time the airship kept its shape. Driven by its popping petrol engine and threshing windmill propeller it took Santos-Dumont at 24 k.p.h. (15 m.p.h.) on a delightful course over the parks and gardens of Paris, and was so safe and manoeuvrable that it convinced him once and for all of the success of his invention. Santos-Dumont became the first man to learn proper flying on a proper flying-machine. At Saint-Cloud he constructed his own aerodrome, with a workshop, hangar and gas plant, and here he built and flew nine more airships of different shapes and sizes.

For all his growing experience, though, it was always a perilous business. Engines burst into flames, cables frayed, valves stuck, gas pressure failed. Once Santos-Dumont crashed into the sixth floor of a hotel and had to be rescued by firemen. Another time he crashed into the top of a tall tree in the Rothschild estate and a Brazilian princess sent a lunch-box up to him. No insurance company would insure him but he survived, learned and tried again. The Paris crowds came to love 'le petit Santos' and his silken bubbles spluttering over the roof-tops.

In 1901, when he was twenty-eight years old, Alberto Santos-Dumont entered for the world's first great air race, the Deutsche Prize. The race was really against the clock, for Santos-Dumont was the only competitor. To win the 125,000-franc prize (worth over £50,000 today) he had to complete a seven-mile circuit round the Eiffel Tower in less than thirty minutes. On 19 October, dressed in flying gear that consisted of a dark suit and a bowler hat tied to his lapels by a cord, the most experienced airship pilot in the world took off in his *No. 6* and in spite of a stiff headwind won the prize with twenty-nine seconds to spare. This was the happiest time in Santos-Dumont's life. He was world famous. Now he became increasingly audacious in the air, increasingly eccentric on the ground.

In his famous *No. 9* – a tubby little runabout with a three horse-power engine and a maximum speed of 24 k.p.h. (15 m.p.h.) – he caused traffic jams wherever he went. He would float down the boulevards at roof-top level, land at a café to join his friends for lunch, or moor outside his flat while he popped inside for a coffee. On Bastille Day in 1903 he appeared in front of a great military review and at a height of 90 metres (300 feet) saluted the President of France, the King of Italy and the French Army with a salvo of twenty-one blank shots from his revolver.

But Santos-Dumont was losing interest in airships. In 1906 he became the first man in Europe to fly an aeroplane and by 1909 he was achieving speeds of 112 k.p.h. (70 m.p.h.) in his beautiful Demoiselle monoplane. Then suddenly, in March 1910, his life suffered a catastrophic change. He abandoned aviation, sold his airships and left Paris for ever. The man who had aroused more enthusiasm for powered flight than any other

man before him never flew again. Suffering from an incurable disease – probably multiple sclerosis – he wandered aimlessly from country to country, a broken man. Finally, desperate, bitter, and prematurely old, he hanged himself by his necktie from the bathroom door, and died. The year was 1922.

3

Santos-Dumont had not been flying his little airships for more than two or three years before rivals began to appear on the scene. He had always been a one-man band and preferred to keep things small and simple. But he was soon overtaken by organized companies who preferred to operate on a much bigger scale. The most important of these rivals was a retired German general called Count Ferdinand von Zeppelin. When, in his sixtieth year, Count Zeppelin formed his first airship company, few were to guess that he would lend his name to one of the most extraordinary flying-machines ever devised by man.

For a number of years it had been known that you could build an airship in two ways – either by elongating an ordinary balloon, as Santos-Dumont had done, or by enclosing an almost limitless number of balloons within a single rigid frame and slinging control car and engines underneath. It was this second type that the Count chose for his first airship, an immense contraption almost 120 metres (400 feet) long. In 1900, before amazed spectators, he lifted his colossal invention, *LZ1* – the first of a great breed – into the skies above Lake Constance. Not surprisingly she

Graf Ferdinand von Zeppelin, the inventor of the Zeppelin airship, in the control car window of one of his early ships.

) Alberto Santos-Dumont became world-famous when n the world's great first air race – round the Eiffel Tower is airship No. 6.

was a failure; she was barely controllable and was scrapped after only three brief flights.

But the old Count was a determined man. With most of his private means gone he ran lotteries to raise more money for more airships. Early failures only doubled his enthusiasm. One ship broke up on the ground. Another caught fire. *LZ5* bumped into a pear-tree and had to have its nose sawn off before it could take off again. But the public acclaimed him in spite of his failures. The King and Queen of Württemberg flew with him. The Kaiser came to greet him when he landed outside Berlin. In 1908 he flew over Switzerland and was cheered down the Rhine by the goggle-eyed populace. In 1909 he formed the world's first commercial passenger airline, called DELAG.

The purpose of the DELAG airline was to ferry passengers between the major cities of Germany. But the Count faced bankruptcy from the beginning. Ship after ship was destroyed by accident – fortunately without any casualties. By 1911 only one ship was left, a new ship called *Schwaben* under the command of a new pilot called Eckener.

In the season of 1912 Dr Hugo Eckener, a graduate in psychology and a former journalist, demonstrated a mastery of the techniques of airship flying that marked a turning point in the Zeppelin story. During that year *Schwaben* carried over 1,500 passengers on more than 200 flights, and her new sister ships – *Victoria Luise, Hansa* and *Sachsen* – did even better. For £50 a go and at 80 k.p.h. (50 m.p.h.) twenty passengers at a time could gulp champagne and gobble caviar while the Fatherland unrolled beneath them. By 1914 nearly 10,000 people had

Hugo Eckener, head of the Zeppelin Company and the world's greatest airshipman, looks down on a German town from the Graf *Zeppelin.*

Leader of Airships, Captain Peter Strasser (right), in the forward control car of an early German Naval Zeppelin (possibly L4) during a flight at the beginning of the Great War.

been carried a total of over 270,000 kilometres (170,000 miles) without anyone receiving even a scratch.

But the Count had really always seen his airships as war machines and the outbreak of the Great War in 1914 was the chance he had been looking for. The Zeppelin company geared itself to the production of airships and the training of crews for the German Naval Airship Division under the command of Captain Peter Strasser. Now the Zeppelin would carry bombs instead of passengers in its belly.

Captain Strasser had a passionate faith in the airship as a military weapon, and was quite convinced his fleet of Zeppelin bombers would bring the war to a speedy end by paralysing Britain's industry and demoralizing Britain's people. He set about improving this new weapon. He fitted more powerful engines and began to use a new light alloy, duralumin, for the rigid structure. He developed aerial bombs and revolving hangars to accommodate the Zeppelins easily whatever the direction of the wind.

(Overleaf) *Giant Zeppelins nose up the Thames during the first Blitz of London. The Germans thought they could win the war by destroying the capital, but in fact they did little damage and suffered heavy casualties. The Zeppelins were easily picked out by searchlights and were no match for high-flying fighter planes firing incendiary bullets.*

Then, on the night of 19 January 1915, the Zeppelin bombers raided England for the first time. In May they bombed London. In June they set Tyneside ablaze in one of the most successful raids of the war. In September, homing in on the reflection of the lights of the world's largest city, they raided London again and started huge fires among the warehouses beyond St Paul's. At first the Londoners had crowded the roof-tops to watch. Now they poured into the underground stations for safety.

The Zeppelin was a powerful psychological weapon but it was not really so devastating as the Germans believed. Because of the difficulties of navigating over an enemy country at night, most of the Zeppelins were miles off target and most of their bombs missed. But the claims of their crews were so exaggerated that Strasser continued to believe he could, with one big knock-out assault on London, win the war for Germany. By 1916 he was adding huge 200 metre (650 foot) super-Zeppelins to his fleet, their undersides blackened to avoid the searchlights, and on 2 September he launched them on the greatest airship raid of the war.

Sixteen giant ships rose into the air from Germany's North Sea bases that night. Never again were so many airships ever to fly in the sky together at one time, for waiting for them in England were two new British weapons – the high-altitude aeroplane and the incendiary bullet. High in the sky some of Strasser's best and bravest crews met a fiery and terrible end. Zeppelin after Zeppelin, ignited by a fighter pilot's bullet, slid slowly down through the sky in a horrifying conflagration. Airmen didn't wear parachutes in those days, but some of them preferred to jump out rather than burn; only two ever survived being shot down.

Strasser refused to give up. To combat the high-flying British fighters he developed Zeppelins of the sub-stratosphere, ships that could carry thirty tons of bombs to a height of 8,000 metres (26,000 feet) at 120 k.p.h. (76 m.p.h.) and in one stroke render the English defence system obsolete. Observation cars were let down on cables, swaying invisibly beneath the clouds while the airship

The wartime Zeppelin L20 got badly lost over Scotland on the night of 2 May 1916 and, after dropping most of its bombs on Craig Castle, Aberdeen, it eventually crash-landed in a Norwegian fjord, where its crew were captured.

remained in hiding above them. But at those high altitudes engines and even compasses froze, and men fell unconscious at their posts from lack of oxygen, or vomited uncontrollably. Blue sparks of static electricity flew out of their fingers and flickered round their fur collars. It was so cold that some of the men wore newspapers under their fur flying-suits, but they still got frost-bite. Sick and exhausted in the strange winds of the upper air, they drifted far from their targets and dropped their bombs harmlessly in the sea and empty fields.

Only one event brightened the gloom for German airshipmen – the remarkable 6,700 kilometre (4,200 mile) flight of *LZ59* to Khartoum and back in an attempt to bring supplies to German forces cut off in East Africa. This was the longest and boldest journey ever made by air up to that time.

Gradually Germany began to replace Zeppelins with aeroplanes for bombing raids. Yet with the war already lost, Strasser still dreamed of smashing London. On 5 August 1918, for the last time, five huge dirigibles headed west for England. In *L70*, the latest and finest of the line, was Strasser himself.

At 9 p.m., approaching the coast of England, Strasser radioed his last command: 'To all airships. Attack according to plan.' That signal was to betray him to the English defences. Within the hour thirteen fighter aircraft had taken off from Yarmouth air station. Among the pilots was Major Egbert Cadbury. He later described his attack on Strasser's ship:

'I approached it from the stern, about 300 feet below it, and fired four drums of explosive ammunition into its stern, which immediately started to light. As I was doing this, one of the other pilots was flying over the top of the Zeppelin and to his horror he saw a man in the machine-gun pit run to the side and jump overboard.'

That fiery pyre was the end of Strasser and the Naval Airship Division. Not long afterwards the war came to an end. As a weapon the Zeppelin had failed – it had done little damage, yet forty per cent of the crews had been killed and only seven out of sixty-eight ships had survived to the end. But as an aircraft it had proved itself beyond any doubt.

Peace brought a world-wide interest in airships and their future seemed sure. The Allies scrambled to loot what Strasser had left behind him. Britain, France and Italy purloined surviving Zeppelins, while America ordered a new one as war reparations.

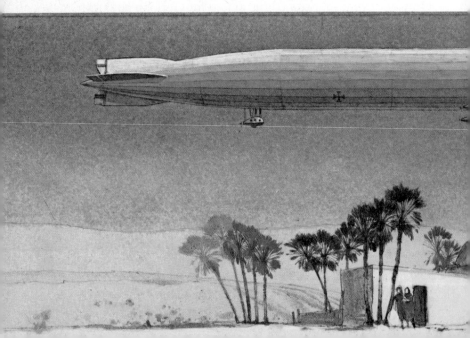

(Left) *In 1919 Major J. Pritchard became the first man to arrive in the New World by air when he parachuted from the R34 to supervize the landing operations. R34 was the first aircraft to make the east-west Atlantic crossing.*

(Below) *In 1917 the Zeppelin L59 flew to beyond Khartoum in the Sudan in an attempt to ferry supplies to German forces in East Africa. By the time it got back to base it had been in the air for nearly 100 hours.*

Keenest in the hunt was Britain. During the war she had mostly confined her use of airships to non-rigid Navy blimps. Altogether nearly 400 of these efficient little craft had seen active service, and they had done sterling work on coastal reconnaissance, submarine and mine spotting, and convoy scouting. No ship in any convoy escorted by them was ever lost through enemy action and they provided a great opportunity for training the crews who were to handle the big rigids of the future.

The British had dabbled in a few experimental rigid airships before the end of the war, but they had seen little service, though the $R29$ had helped in the sinking of a German U-boat in the last weeks of the war. After the war the British decided to continue with their programme of military rigids, and one of these – the 192 metre, 57,000 cubic metre, 100 k.p.h. (643 foot, two million cubic foot, 65 m.p.h.) airship $R34$, a copy of a captured German Zeppelin, $L33$ – became famous as the first airship ever to cross the Atlantic and the first aircraft of any kind to fly the Atlantic east to west and in both directions.

Two weeks before $R34$ set off, however, two British fliers, Alcock and Brown, made the first direct non-stop crossing of the Atlantic west to east in an old wartime bomber, and this robbed the airship of some of the glory. But the ship's performance was impressive enough. In the early hours of the morning of 2 July 1919 it left East Fortune in Scotland at the start of its epoch-making flight to the New World with a crew of thirty, a general, a kitten and a stowaway on board, under the command of Major G. H. Scott. 108 hours later, dangerously low on fuel but other-wise untroubled, it reached Mineola airfield, New York, and after three days of festivities in America returned, again untroubled, in seventy-five hours. During that pioneer double crossing $R34$ learnt a lot about air navigation, radio communications and Atlantic meteorology. It had pointed the way. Others were soon to follow.

America started to build another copy of another captured Zeppelin, $L49$, and called it *Shenandoah* – 'Daughter of the Stars'.

In 1923 it was commissioned as a ship of the U.S. Navy, and in 1924 it was joined by a sister ship, *Los Angeles*, built by Dr Eckener's Zeppelin company as war reparations. Filled with safe, non-inflammable helium gas (which could only be obtained in America at that time), *Los Angeles* proved to be one of the finest airships in history, and in the next seven years she flew a total of 331 flights and 5,000 hours in the air, successfully taking part in many fleet manoeuvres and military experiments.

Clearly, airships worked. By comparison, aeroplanes were still noisy, small, short-range 'crates'. But what to do with them? Clever people had bold ideas. The airship, with its range and endurance, was surely the vehicle with which to conduct the exploration of the unknown surfaces of the earth.

5

Only fifty years ago the white desert of the Arctic was an unknown world. Was it sea or was it land? No one knew. One of the best ways of finding out was from the air.

The idea wasn't new. In 1897 a young Swede called Andrée, with two companions, had tried to float across the North Pole by balloon, and failed. In 1907 an American called Wellman tried it by airship and failed. In 1925 the Norwegian explorer Roald Amundsen, the first man to reach the South Pole, tried to reach the North Pole by aeroplane and failed. Undeterred, he tried it again – this time by airship. An American millionaire called Lincoln Ellsworth put up the money and an Italian airship designer called Umberto Nobile agreed to pilot the airship, a small semi-rigid of his own design called the *Norge*.

The flight of the *Norge* was to prove one of the most enterprising and successful in the history of airships. On 11 May 1926, with sixteen men and Nobile's dog Titina on board, the *Norge* cast off from its base at King's Bay, Spitzbergen, and

General Umberto Nobile

headed north towards the Pole and the unknown world beyond.

Inside the cabin it was noisy, cold and cramped. They had forgotten to bring any drinking water, so they drank tepid coffee out of dozens of broken thermos flasks instead. There were only two seats and Amundsen's enormous feet, clad in grass-stuffed boots, took up a lot of room. But they pressed forward over the fractured and hummocked ice of the Arctic wilderness and on 12 May they reached the North Pole. Then they found themselves flying across a void of frozen seas no human eye had ever seen, to Alaska on the other side of the world. Here, tossed between Alaska and Siberia by violent winds, they made a wild and dangerous flight through fog before Nobile brought the airship safely down on the ice at Teller near Nome under the gaze of a group of startled Eskimoes. They had crossed the world from the Mediterranean to the Pacific via the North Pole. In three days they had made the first crossing of the Arctic and discovered a frozen ocean in a region hitherto inaccessible to man. It was the greatest feat of aerial exploration up to that time.

Amundsen, as leader of the expedition, claimed credit for the success of the *Norge* flight. But it was Nobile, as commander of the airship, who finally got it. His success led him to try it again. He had explored 130,000 square kilometres (50,000 square miles) of the Arctic in the *Norge*. Now he aimed to explore the remaining four million ($1\frac{1}{2}$ million square miles) in a new airship called the *Italia*. 'Perhaps,' said Mussolini, the dictator of Italy, 'it would be better not to tempt fate a second time.' 'Let him go,' said Balbo, the Air Minister, who was jealous of Nobile and hated airships, 'he can't possibly return to trouble us again.'

And so Nobile went. On 15 May 1928 *Italia* set out from King's Bay on its first flight of exploration into unknown territory beyond Franz Joseph Land. Sixty-nine hours later it returned to base safe and sound. All seemed well, but all was not. The spring weather was unexpectedly bad. There were nasty winds and freezing fogs and the *Italia* iced up more heavily than the *Norge*. But Nobile wasted no time preparing for the next flight.

The Italia *nestles in her hangar at King's Bay before her ill-fated flight in 1928.*

By 23 May all was ready and *Italia* was walked out of its special hangar for the last time. They blessed the oak cross the Pope had given them and then they set off, sixteen scientists, journalists and airshipmen, and the dog Titina, in an attempt to reach the North Pole by a different route. For seven of them it was their second flight to the Pole in two years. For eight of them it was to be a flight of no return.

Italia had taken off at 4.28 a.m. At twenty minutes past midnight the next morning, helped by a strong following wind, she reached the roof of the world, the North Pole. Slowly the ship turned over the exact geographical zero and Nobile leaned out and dropped the flag of Italy and the large oaken cross. Excitedly he radioed his triumph to the Pope, to Mussolini and the world.

But the success was short-lived. Even in May the Arctic could be treacherous. Strong headwinds lashed against *Italia* as she struggled to regain base. It became difficult to steer a straight course. Fog hampered navigation. Fuel lines were choked. An ominous coating of ice began to form on the outside of the wallowing ship and the propellers shot bits of it like bullets into the hull. For twenty-four hours they flew through fog and driving snow, barely making 40 k.p.h. (25 m.p.h.) against increasing headwinds, and soon they were lost. Then the elevators – the tail planes that controlled the up-and-down movement of the ship – seized up with ice and the *Italia* dived towards the frozen plains below.

'Stop the engines!' yelled Nobile. The ship was light. She began to rise. She rose through the clouds into the sunlight above them. Now they could repair the elevators and take navigational sightings. They were at least 160 kilometres (100 miles) off course and several hundred miles from base – helpless in a desert of ice. Worse, they were now at pressure height and blowing off gas, and the warm sun caused them to blow off more. When they came down below the clouds again they became heavier, and the cold made them heavier still. Remorselessly the ship sank towards the jagged ice pack below. They braced themselves for the shock. The ice loomed up like great blocks of concrete.

The impact tore the control car right out of the ship and left ten men and one small dog stranded on the ice. One was dead, some – like Nobile, whose leg was broken – were injured. Six were left in the hull of the doomed ship as it drifted helplessly back towards the Pole. They were never seen again. For the men left shocked and battered on the lonely ice, only a few provisions, a small tent and a miraculously unbroken radio lay between them and death. It was the radio, bleeping out its pathetic and desperate signal, 'SOS ITALIA...SOS ITALIA', that finally informed the world of their predicament and set in motion the greatest Arctic rescue operation in history.

On the ice the survivors waited. Morale rose when they shot a polar-bear for meat – at least they wouldn't starve to death. But there were days and days without sun or hope. Then, on 6 June, a fortnight after the crash, they picked up a radio message: 'The Soviet Embassy has informed the Italian Government that an

The Norge *takes off from King's Bay, Spitzbergen, on 11 May 1926 on her flight to the North Pole and beyond. Note the large ground crew to handle the ship before departure.*

General Nobile's dog, Titina, went with him on all his polar flights and was rescued alive and well after the crash.

SOS from the *Italia* has been picked up by a young Soviet farmer, Nicholas Schmidt, at Archangel on 3 June.' The jubilant air-shipmen dyed their tent red to make it easier for rescuers to see, and sat and waited.

The rescue operation was an international affair in which eight nations sent ships and planes to search the Arctic. But more than two weeks passed before the first plane spotted the red tent and by then the sea was melting all around it. On 23 June a Swedish pilot called Lundborg managed to land his skiplane on the ice near the tent. He had strict instructions, he said, to rescue Nobile first so that he could help them look for the others. Nobile protested that as captain he should be taken off last. But he was overruled.

Eventually, after several more desperate adventures, the remainder of the *Italia*'s survivors, including the dog Titina, were rescued by a Russian icebreaker. They had been on the ice for forty-nine days. Altogether eight airshipmen – half the total crew – lost their lives. So did some of the rescuers – among them Nobile's companion on the *Norge*, Roald Amundsen, who was lost without trace after setting out on an air search.

(Overleaf) *The remaining survivors of the* Italia *catastrophe by the red tent where they were found by the Russian ice-breaker* Krassin *after the biggest Arctic rescue operation in history. The overturned ski-plane had already rescued Nobile but crashed when it returned to pick up his men.*

23

The end of Nobile's ordeal in the Arctic was the beginning of a far more terrible ordeal in Italy. His enemies spread malicious rumours that by allowing himself to be rescued first he had deserted his post and his men. It was hinted that one of his officers was guilty of cannibalism. In any case, Nobile had lost his ship and was blamed for it. In disgust he left his homeland for voluntary exile in the Soviet Union. He built more airships and went on another Arctic expedition. But many more years were to pass before the value of his achievements became clear.

In 1958 the American submarine *Nautilus* crossed the Arctic Ocean, submerged, from Alaska to Spitzbergen via the North Pole, following the same route as Nobile's *Norge* but in the opposite direction. Afterwards the submarine's captain wrote to Nobile: 'From your courageous flight over the Polar pack ice in 1926 it was established that there was no land between Alaska and Spitzbergen. Without this knowledge, found by you and confirmed by the aerial expeditions that followed you, we would not have known enough to undertake this voyage.'

General Nobile is still alive. He is over eighty now but he still remembers the *Italia* tragedy with bitterness.

The *Italia* was not the only airship to have been lost. In 1919 the American Navy had placed an order for a British airship of novel design. In the summer of 1921 this ship, the *R38*, on her final trials over Hull, was put through violent man-oeuvrings at full speed and low altitude. Her designers hadn't made allowance for aerodynamic stresses, however, and the *R38* broke in two and fell in flames into the River Humber. All but one of the American crew and most of the leading British airshipmen of the time were killed.

Two years later the French rigid *Dixmude*, during a flight to the Sahara, was lost with all hands over the Mediterranean, so ending French involvement in rigid airships. In April 1925 the British rigid *R33* came near to disaster when it was torn from its mast in a gale and driven backwards across the North Sea to Holland before its skeleton crew could regain control. Later in the same year the U.S. Navy airship *Shenandoah*, under her experienced commander Zachary Lansdowne, was ordered against his better judgement to fly to the Middle West across a region notorious for its ferocious squalls. Towards dawn the next day the ship was struck by a tremendous storm. Her keel snapped, her bow broke off and her control car plummeted to earth over Ohio. An hour later a buoyant section of the hull, flown like a free balloon, landed safely, but out of the airship's total crew of forty-three, only fourteen survived.

These accidents occurred as a result of human error or freak weather – not because there was something basically wrong with airships. In the hands of experts like Dr Hugo Eckener, chief of the German Zeppelin Company, and his highly experienced ex-wartime airship personnel like Captains Lehmann, Schiller, Flemming and Pruss, the airship could prove as safe as an ocean liner. And in September 1928, to demonstrate the possibilities of commercial airship travel around the world, Eckener launched the most famous and best-loved airship ever built, the slender and beautiful *LZ126* – christened *Graf Zeppelin* in honour of the old Count's ninetieth birthday.

Graf Zeppelin was 230 metres (755 feet) long, 85,000 cubic metres (three million cubic feet) in capacity, and capable of cruising at about 120 k.p.h. (75 m.p.h.). She was a big ship, but not half as big as Eckener would have liked if he had had the money, for she could only carry twenty passengers in addition to her crew. However, they travelled in luxury hitherto unknown in aircraft, with ten cosy cabins to sleep in and a plush little wine-red lounge to sit and dine and watch the world go by below.

Eckener always regarded the *Graf Zeppelin* as the guinea-pig of airship travel, a trail-blazing training ship rather than the flagship of the fleet. But he was a great showman and publicist as well as a great airshipman. In the face of increasing competition from the

Air travel has never been so comfortable and luxurious as it was on board the Graf Zeppelin and the Hindenburg. (Left) A double sleeping cabin on the Graf Zeppelin and (right) the lounge and promenade deck on the Hindenburg with large picture windows looking down on the world below.

aeroplane he took his new ship on a series of spectacular proving flights that caught the imagination of the world and made the *Graf Zeppelin* a household word.

In October 1928 the ship made an eventful maiden flight to America. Halfway across the Atlantic she was struck by severe squalls which sent her crockery flying and tore the fabric of one of her stabilizing fins. A team of men who didn't mind heights volunteered to climb out in mid-air and patch the tear in a 80 k.p.h. (50 m.p.h.) slipstream, but for some hours the world

(Right) In 1929 the Graf Zeppelin became the first aircraft to fly round the world. Crossing the vast unknown wilderness of Siberia on her way to Japan, the great ship caused panic among the inhabitants of the remote villages.

(Left) The all electric kitchen of the Graf Zeppelin and (right) the dining room of the Hindenburg.

feared for the airship's safety. On the return flight the ship was struck by a Force 11 gale and blown 480 kilometres (300 miles) off course, at one time travelling backwards at 32 k.p.h. (20 m.p.h.). But eventually she made the French coast safely, having proved she could ride out the very worst kind of weather the Atlantic could deal her.

Next the *Graf* made another proving flight, the most fabulous it was possible to make in Europe. On the first day of spring in 1929 she voyaged along the Riviera and over the Vatican, Vesuvius and Capri. The passengers had a dinner of turtle soup, ham with asparagus, roast beef, rich cakes and fine wines over the Ionian Sea, breakfast over Crete and lunch over Palestine. They flew below sea level in the Dead Sea and in moonlight over Jerusalem. They floated down the coast of Egypt, drifted past Mount Olympus covered in snow, and after a difficult crossing of the Alps landed safely home after eighty-one hours in the air.

Graf Zeppelin looked good, handled well and felt safe. From now on triumph followed triumph and in the summer of 1929 Hugo Eckener took her on one of the most splendid aerial voyages ever made by any kind of aircraft at any time. For on 1 August he took off from Friedrichshafen at the start of the first-ever passenger flight round the world. In America he picked up his distinguished passengers and from there he flew eastwards back to Germany and from Germany eastwards to the Soviet Union and beyond.

The ship, like a silver fish, swam over the immense open spaces of Russia, where huge forest fires started by lonely hunters and prospectors reduced visibility to a hundred yards and made navigation difficult. They flew over the Urals and descended from Europe into Asia – a terrifying and utterly desolate landscape of trackless wastes between the Ob and the Yenisei where swamps blazed with flowers and the primitive inhabitants of the remote villages fled in panic at the approach of the huge monster in the sky. At night they looked out on a moon like an enormous yellow ball on the southern horizon, while the sun hung just below the northern horizon and the sky glowed brightly all through that uncanny night. By dawn they were over the frontier town of Yakutsk on the River Lena, in the midst of the mysterious vastness of Siberia, and soon they were flying over country no human eye had seen before. Anxiously they climbed the uncharted 1,800 metre (6,000 foot) Stanovoi Mountains, sliding through a pass with 45 metres (150 feet) to spare, before they caught their first sight of the vivid blue of the Pacific on the other side.

In four days *Graf Zeppelin* reached Japan, a journey that normally took four weeks by boat or two weeks by railway. Then from Japan she floated across the Pacific to Los Angeles and from Los Angeles across the continent of America to Lakehurst and New York and a reception few aircraft and few airmen have ever met. In 21 days, 5 hours, 31 minutes, *Graf Zeppelin* and her eighty passengers and crew had encircled the earth in perfect comfort and safety. 'I thought the day of the great adventurers like Columbus, Vasco da Gama and Magellan was past,' President Hoover of the U.S.A. told Eckener when they met. 'Now I know such an adventurer is in my presence.'

By now the whole idea of ocean flying had been accepted. The *Graf* flew on publicity trips to almost every capital city of Europe and even to the remote regions of the Taimyr Peninsula and Novaya Zemlya in the Arctic. In 1930 she started on a scheduled passenger and mail service between Germany and Brazil and Eckener was invited to consider an airship service between Holland and the East Indies. Draughtsmen worked on futuristic designs for the sophisticated airships of the future.

But the only other country to follow Germany's lead with commercial passenger airships was Britain, and the year 1930, the year *Graf Zeppelin* started its routine South America run, saw the brief triumph of the *R100* and the desperate tragedy of the *R101*.

The British airship R100 rides at her mooring mast in Montreal after her successful proving flight across the Atlantic in 1930.

7

The *R101* was the biggest airship ever built in Britain. In 1930, on its proving flight to India, it crashed and burned in the worst British air disaster up to that time. Most of the leading airshipmen of Britain were killed and no British rigid airship ever flew again.

The story of *R101* is a tragedy of errors. It really began in 1924, when the British Government approved a scheme known as the British Imperial Airship Programme. The purpose of this scheme was to set up a world-wide air transport network by means of a fleet of giant airships operating between the major cities of the British Empire. The aeroplanes of those days were still not capable of carrying commercial passengers over such vast distances with any great speed or comfort, but the British reckoned their airships would be able to carry ten tons of mail and 150 passengers to India, Australia, Canada and South Africa with all the comfort and luxury of an ocean liner but in a fifth of the time – three days to India instead of three weeks, two weeks for the round trip to Australia instead of two or three months.

But airships in Britain had many critics. The huge, unwieldy dirigibles were at the mercy of the weather, they said; headwinds slowed them down in the air, squalls endangered them on the ground, so how could they keep to a timetable, how could they guarantee safety? Airships were as big as steamships yet they couldn't carry much more than lorries, so how could they pay their way, how could they ever be commercially worthwhile?

The British Government decided to proceed as carefully and as thoroughly as possible, and proposed to start with two experimental airships. These were to be bigger than any airship ever built so far; they were to have a gas capacity of 140,000 cubic metres (five million cubic feet) – a third more than the *Graf Zeppelin* – and be able to carry up to sixty tons, including luxury accommodation for one hundred passengers. One ship, the so-called 'capitalist' ship *R100*, was to be built by private enterprise and make a proving flight to Canada. The other ship, the so-called

'Socialist' ship *R101*, was to be built by the State and make a proving flight to India.

Slowly the rival ships began to take shape. Eventually it was *R100* that was ready to leave England first. She had been designed by Dr Barnes Wallis, who later became famous as the inventor of the Dambusters' bouncing bomb in the Second World War, and in her way she was an engineering triumph – the simplest rigid airship ever built, with a main hull made up of only fifty-two standard parts, compared with many thousands in *R101*. In the summer of 1930 she made her successful proving flight to Canada and back under the command of Wing-Commander Ralph Booth. But *R101* was still far from ready for her trail-blazing flight to India or anywhere else.

The trouble with *R101* was that she was too complicated. During her construction in the huge hangar at Cardington she had absorbed 3 kilometres (2 miles) of girders, 10 kilometres (6 miles) of booms, 16 kilometres (11 miles) of cable, 24 kilometres (15 miles) of rods, 56 kilometres (35 miles) of tubing and the intestinal membranes of one million oxen to provide the material (known as goldbeaters' skin) for the airship's gas bags. These sort of requirements were fairly normal for big rigid airships. But the designer of *R101* wanted to make his ship the best and most modern in the world and he tried out so many new-fangled, half-developed ideas that in the end they proved the ship's undoing. The valves stuck, the gas bags punctured, and the special diesel engines, the extra-strong airframe, the sophisticated servo steering gear and other clever but weighty items made the ship heavy. When *R101* was tried out she was found to be overweight and underpowered. She couldn't fly high enough or fast enough and she went into unpredictable dives. She could only lift thirty-five tons, not sixty, and this wasn't enough for a long-distance flight to the tropics. She was a beautiful-looking airship but she was a bad one. At the last minute she was sliced in half and a new gas bag was inserted to give the ship more lift. Now she was 233 metres (777 feet) long –

as long as an ocean liner. But the airframe kept puncturing the gas bags and the outer cover rotted and split, exposing the vulnerable gas bags to further damage by wind and rain. It became increasingly clear that the ship was not going to be ready for her great demonstration flight to India, now scheduled for the end of September 1930.

At this very tricky point came disastrous intervention from outside. Lord Thomson, the Air Minister, intended to fly to India and back in *R101*. He had hopes of becoming Viceroy of India and thought his prestige would be greatly enhanced by arriving in the country of his ambition in this sensational way. Publicly he put the airship's safety first, but privately he put his own ambitions first. 'I must insist on the programme for the Indian flight being adhered to,' he told the *R101* team, 'as I have made my plans accordingly.' When the September departure date was postponed he was furious. When the Director of Civil Aviation, backed by the Director of Airship Development, pointed out that the ship was not yet in an airworthy condition for such a long journey, the Air Minister refused to listen. The *R101*, he once said, was as safe as a house – except for the millionth chance. And he insisted that that chance be taken – at the same time taking out extra insurance for himself and his valet.

So, on Saturday 4 October 1930, the great silver ship rode at its mooring mast at Cardington for the last time while passengers and stores were taken on board. At 7.30 that evening she finally cast off for Egypt and India under the command of Flight-Lieutenant Carmichael Irwin, but she was so weighed down with fuel, ballast, men and official luxuries like thick pile carpets, champagne and Lord Thomson's voluminous baggage, that at first she staggered and sank under the load. Then she turned and headed through the black wet night towards the Channel – into the teeth of a freshening wind and a gathering storm.

The weather forecast was bad. *R101* had never flown in bad weather. She had never done her high-speed trials or her forty-eight hour endurance test and her Certificate of Airworthiness

The skeleton of the R101 the morning after the crash. The bodies are being laid out under white sheets at the edge of the wood on the right.

was a sham. On that fatal night the ship had great difficulty in gaining any height and the engines could make only feeble headway against the gale. But to those on board everything seemed to be under control and over London the Air Minister and most of the leading airshipmen of Britain sat down to their last supper. At midnight the airship radioed Cardington: 'After an excellent supper our distinguished passengers smoked a final cigar, and, having sighted the French coast, have now gone to bed to rest after the excitement of their final leave-taking. The crew have settled down to watch-keeping routine.' It was the last signal of any length ever sent by *R101*.

At 2 a.m., approaching Beauvais in northern France, the ship's watch was changed. It was pitch black outside and the wind was roaring and the rain beating down. Suddenly one of the crew, peering down, shouted out in astonishment: 'We're nearly at roof level!' The ship was now flying at less than half her length from the ground. Only a few feet below them they caught a glimpse of the spire of Beauvais Cathedral. *R101* was so low that she woke up the inhabitants of the town. They hurried into the streets and saw the huge ship, red and green navigation lights glowing, wallow broadside above them before sinking out of sight behind the roof-tops. Then the men on watch on board *R101* felt the ship go into a steep dive. The ship recovered but though the elevators were in the hard-up position they were no longer responding. In the control car they already knew they were going to crash. The bows of the ship were unaccountably heavy. The ship dived a second time. Another dive was bound to come. The captain signalled 'slow' to the engine cars. The Chief Coxswain rushed aft to warn the crew. 'We're down, lads!' he yelled. 'We're down!'

A French rabbit-catcher was setting snares near the edge of a wood when he saw the giant airship wobble and then dive straight at him. She hit the ground in front of him with a crunch and skidded for fifty-five metres (sixty yards) before coming to a halt. For a moment nothing happened. The men in the control car got ready for an emergency exit. But suddenly there was an immense explosion and a vast white fire lit up the sky as 140,000 cubic metres (five million cubic feet) of hydrogen gas ignited. The rabbit-catcher saw human figures running like madmen in the flames and then he turned and fled in terror into the woods.

Eight of the crew managed to get out of the fire, and six of these survived. The rest of the men, all the officers, and all the

(Right) *A few hours after setting off on her maiden flight to India the* R101 *was forced down into a hillside near Beauvais, France. Seconds later she burst into flames. Only six of her crew survived.*

(Below) *Three survivors of the* R101 *crash (Binks, Bell and Leech) follow the carriage carrying the remains of their comrades through the streets of Beauvais.*

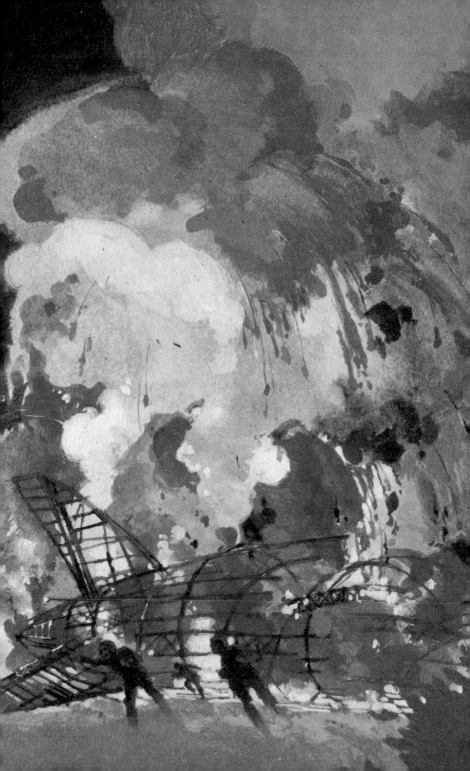

passengers, including Lord Thomson, were burnt beyond recognition. In all forty-eight men lost their lives in *R101*.

In Britain there was a State funeral for the victims and the nation was plunged into mourning. The public turned against airships and the Government stopped any further development of them. *R100* was sold for scrap for £450. Plans for the huge *R102* were abandoned. No British airship ever flew again.

The Court of Enquiry found that the probable reason for the disaster was a large tear in the outer cover of the airship caused by severe turbulence over the coast of France. This in turn probably led to a sudden deflation of the forward gas cells, making the ship extremely heavy in the bows. *R101* was then probably forced down by a violent downdraught she no longer had any means of resisting.

To anyone who knew the story of the development of His Majesty's Airship *R101*, this finding would have come as no surprise.

Now the pace of disaster was quickening. Of the four nations that had once flown rigid airships, only two were left – America and Germany. In the year following the loss of *R101* the Americans launched their latest rigid, *Akron*, a splendid Navy airship which could carry 270 people (a record) and five fighter aircraft for 16,000 kilometres (10,000 miles) without refuelling. But less than two years after her first flight, the ship was recklessly flown into a storm off New Jersey and forced down into the sea with the loss of seventy-three lives. Three weeks later, *Akron's* sister ship, *Macon*, made her first flight. But in February 1935, while taking part in naval manoeuvres over the Pacific, the ship ran into severe turbulence and had to crash-land off the coast of California when the tail structure began to break up. Eighty-three men got out safely but the airship was lost. Now only Germany was left.

By the end of 1935 *Graf Zeppelin* had made over 500 flights and more than 100 Atlantic crossings, mostly to Brazil. She had flown nearly a million miles and carried almost 12,000 passengers. In spite of the disasters that had befallen other airships, this one remained as popular as ever with the public and rarely flew with an empty berth on board. The *Graf Zeppelin* was one of the world's most successful aircraft, but Hugo Eckener was well aware that she was really far too small. What he had always wanted was a much bigger and a much faster ship that could carry more passengers in greater comfort and safety. And at the end of 1935 he was able to finish building just such a ship. She was the best and biggest airship ever to fly people across the ocean. She was also the last. Her name was *Hindenburg*.

Hindenburg was 240 metres (803 feet) long – only a little shorter than the *Queen Mary*, the biggest liner afloat. Her gas capacity was 200,000 cubic metres (seven million cubic feet), almost double that of the *Graf Zeppelin*, and her cruising speed of 136 k.p.h. (85 m.p.h.) was a good 16 k.p.h. (10 m.p.h.) faster. In luxury she was unmatched. Housed entirely inside the hull were twenty-five double-berth cabins to accommodate fifty passengers, each cabin fitted with a writing table and hot and cold running water. On either side were the public rooms – a dining saloon to port, tables laid with fresh flowers and silver, comfortable lounge and writing-room to starboard, and promenades with large picture-windows looking down on the world passing by only a few hundred feet below. There was a fireproofed smoking-room, a reading- and writing-room, a shower and all-electric galley. High in the sky you could play on a special lightweight piano, dance on the dance-floor, browse through the library, visit the doctor and attend Mass on Sunday. For an incomparable form of travel you paid £86 single between Frankfurt, Germany, and Lakehurst, U.S.A.

There was only one snag – she didn't have the right gas. Dr Eckener had done everything possible to make *Hindenburg* the safest airship ever built and all along he had intended to inflate her with helium. But in the end the U.S.A. refused to supply

Germany with the helium and so into the largest aircraft ever built Eckener was forced to put inflammable and explosive hydrogen.

The *Hindenburg* made her maiden flight in March 1936. Against Eckener's will her tail was painted with swastikas and she was forced to join the *Graf Zeppelin* on a propaganda tour of Germany on behalf of Adolf Hitler and the Nazi Party. That summer she made several fast ocean crossings to Rio and New York and in the spring of 1937 nine more cabins were installed, enabling the ship to carry a total of seventy passengers. On 4 May *Hindenburg* left Frankfurt with ninety-seven people on board, thirty-six of them passengers, for the first flight of the season and the last of her life.

At 7 p.m. on 6 May 1937, after some delay due to stormy weather conditions, Captain Max Pruss, commander of the *Hindenburg*, began his approach to the landing-field at Lakehurst. At 7.25 the mooring lines came down from the bow and the ship hung motionless twenty metres (seventy-five feet) above the ground while her passengers stood by the promenade windows waving to friends and relations below. Then a blue flame – probably St Elmo's fire, a form of static electricity – shot along the top of the ship near the tail. Almost certainly it ignited a dangerous mixture of air and escaping hydrogen, for there was a sudden flash and a huge mushroom of white fire billowed out of the stern. Within seconds the flames had shot through the whole ship as gas cell after gas cell exploded. The

Minutes before tragedy, the world's commercial passenger airship arrives over New York after her 21st crossing of the Atlantic.

stern hit the ground, the bow rose 150 metres (500 feet) into the air and fell slowly, bouncing once, an incandescent mass of crumbling wreckage. Human figures leapt from the furnace, some on fire, some miraculously unscathed. A minute later it was all over.

Sixty-two people survived out of the ninety-seven on board. Thirteen passengers and twenty-two crew perished, including Captain Ernst Lehmann, Director of Zeppelin Flight Operations and one of the world's most experienced airship commanders, who died of burns several hours later.

No passenger Zeppelin ever flew again. The *LZ126*, *Graf Zeppelin*, which was returning from Rio under Captain Hans Schiller when *Hindenburg* blew up, completed its last flight and was grounded. *LZ130*, *Graf Zeppelin II* – *Hindenburg's* sister ship – was completed in 1938 and made a few training flights. But America again refused to supply Germany with helium and in

The finest airship ever built, the Hindenburg, *caught fire while landing at Lakehurst, New Jersey, on 6 May 1937. It was a small air disaster by today's standards, but it spelled the end of the big rigid airships.*

1940, on the orders of Air-Marshal Goering, both the Zeppelins were broken up and their hangar destroyed.

Even if *Hindenburg* had never caught fire, this is how the story of the great airships was bound to end. For the world was now at war – a war that would be fought in the air by Spitfires and Messerschmidts, Flying Fortresses and flying-bombs. In such a war there was no longer any room for the slow-flying, low-flying, gas-filled Zeppelins. It was the end of an era.

9 Fortunately the end of the rigids was not the end of airships altogether. A number of U.S. Navy blimp squadrons were formed when America entered the Second World War and these soon saw service as convoy escorts and submarine scouts in the Pacific, Atlantic, Caribbean and Mediterranean, with bases as far afield as Trinidad, Brazil and Morocco. 135 of these wartime blimps were built and they did well. Some of them flew all the way across the Atlantic, the first blimps ever to do so. One of them was actually involved in a remarkable shoot-out with a German submarine off the coast of Florida, and was shot down before the submarine dived.* Altogether they escorted 89,000 merchant ships through coastal waters and not a ship was lost while they were in attendance.

After the war the U.S. Navy airships took on a different role. In 1956 they became part of the early warning radar network of the North American Air Defense system. They were much bigger than the wartime blimps and they repeatedly broke air endurance records. In 1957 the *ZPG2* airship *Snowbird* under Cdr J. R. Hunt flew across the Atlantic to Portugal, then down the west coast of Africa and back across the Atlantic to Florida non-stop – a distance of 15,260 kilometres (8,261 nautical miles)

*One of the airshipmen was killed by a shark, the others were rescued. The U-boat was later sunk by a surface ship.

in 11 days, 14 minutes, 18 seconds spent entirely in the air. In 1958 another *ZPG2* flew 14,400 kilometres (9,000 miles) to deliver supplies to a scientific expedition deep in the Canadian Arctic, and in the same year the biggest blimp ever built – the 120 metre long, 43,000 cubic metre (403 foot, 1,500,000 cubic foot) capacity *ZPG3W* – made its maiden flight. But improved early warning radar stations began to replace the Navy airships. One by one they were decommissioned and in 1964 the last Airship Group of the United States Navy was disbanded.

Today Goodyear operate several civilian blimps for goodwill flights and public service advertising in America, together with one airship, the *Europa*, in Europe. At the time of writing one small advertising blimp flies in Germany, another in Japan. More commercial blimps are planned and several tiny private ones are on the stocks. It seems impossible there won't be more. They are handy, safe and fun. They are fascinating to watch and delightful to fly in. They are also useful. Scientists can use them to survey game herds, whale schools, mineral deposits and archaeological sites. Government officials can use them to spot sea pollution, land erosion and crop disease. TV stations, photographers, traffic police and town planners can use them in ways they can't use planes or helicopters.

'Buoyant flight,' the experts say, 'is the application of a physical principle and physical principles do not become obsolete.' The small, non-rigid airship is on the way back. But what about the big rigid?

The end of the Zeppelins marked the end of the last big rigids, the end of a saga that had lasted forty years. In their brief career they had enjoyed many triumphs and endured many tragedies. They had pioneered aerial navigation

(Overleaf) *Airships are far from dead. In this artist's impression of the future, a large double-hulled cargo-carrier lifts a prefabricated building into place. Airships could play a vital part in the development of remote areas.*

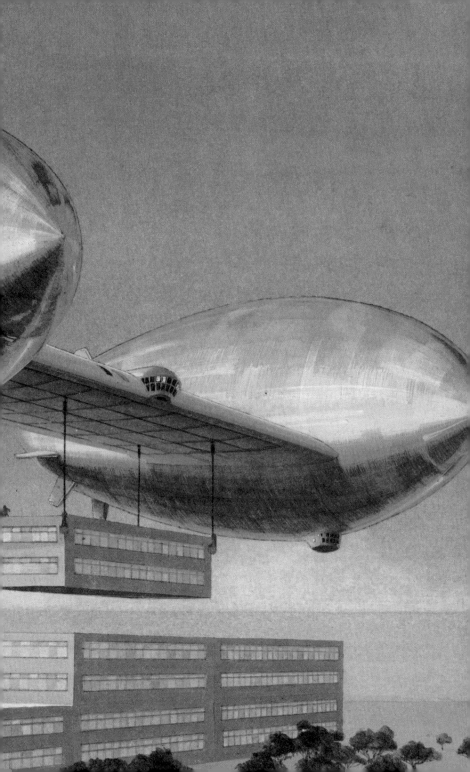

and intercontinental air transport and made a lasting contribution to human progress. Future airmen benefited from what these airshipmen discovered in the skies around the earth.

So what went wrong? In the early years of the twentieth century it had always seemed that powered flight would develop along two different but parallel lines – on the one hand, the heavier-than-air aeroplane, on the other the lighter-than-air airship. In those days there was room for both. They were not rivals, for what one could do the other could not, and vice versa.

If in the end the big rigid appeared to fail, it was not because there was something basically wrong with the concept. It was not an inherently dangerous invention but an inherently safe one. It was not too big but too small. It was not old-fashioned but ahead of its time. It failed for a variety of causes that are now avoidable – lack of information about weather, bad technology, pilot error due to inexperience, inflammable hydrogen gas. Eventually these causes could have been ironed out. But there was no time. The Second World War put an end to rigid airships once and for all.

Technology has taken huge strides since then. Today a big airship could avail itself of an up-to-the-minute world-wide weather service. It could avail itself of vastly improved techniques and materials, including computers for the design calculations, nuclear power for the engines, and ultra-light, ultra-strong plastics, alloys and carbon fibres for the structure. Above all it could avail itself of safe, non-inflammable helium gas. Today from a technical point of view there is nothing to stop anyone building a big, strong, safe, efficient rigid airship.

The real problem now is economic – can an airship be an economic proposition? Can it pay? It is unlikely that future rigids will ever be major passenger carriers – they would be no cheaper than a jumbo jet and five times slower. But as a long-distance cargo carrier, especially of bulky, prefabricated loads, they would seem to have very good prospects. How else could you deliver, say, a bridge, or a boiler, or an oil derrick, or a transformer, or a generator, straight from the factory direct to the work site 3,000 kilometres (2,000 miles) or so away in less than twenty-four hours? Planes and helicopters couldn't do it, because the bigger you build them the heavier they become and the less load they can carry. The opposite is true of airships. The bigger they are the more efficient they become.

Airships have other advantages. Unlike aeroplanes they don't pollute the atmosphere. They are not a noise nuisance. They need only a fraction of the power a plane needs because they don't need power to keep themselves up. They don't need vast tracts of land for airports. They are less liable to mid-air collisions. They are not bound to crash to their doom when the engines fail. They can hold off, stop in mid-air or fly backwards out of danger. And when the day comes when there is no more petrol left in the world and the last aeroplane is grounded, the airship can go nuclear and keep flying.

At present the airship is undergoing something of a revival. America, for example, has made a design study for a nuclear rigid of 357,000 cubic metres (12,500,000 cubic feet) which could carry 500 people and circle the earth repeatedly without refuelling. Russia talks of 480 k.p.h. (300 m.p.h.) rigids to help develop natural resources in the wilds of Siberia. Germany contemplates a revival of the Zeppelin passenger service to America, while in Britain a commercial company is continuing with its plans to develop a large rigid airship to carry cargo, and the Shell Oil Company is designing a colossal 540 metre long, three million cubic metre (1,800 foot, 100 million cubic foot) capacity ship to airlift natural gas from the Sahara.

So are airships going to be a major transport system of the future? Will we one day see these great ships chug by in the sky again? Or will they remain the most promising failure in the whole history of manned flight?

Who knows?

The aeroplane is a heavier-than-air craft and can only fly as a result of aerodynamic lift – i.e. the lifting effect of the air flow over the wings, caused by the aeroplane being propelled forward by its engines. The airship, on the other hand, is able to fly mainly as a result of aerostatic lift i.e. when it is inflated with a gas that is lighter than air (e.g. helium or hydrogen), or even with hot air (which is lighter than cold air), it becomes buoyant and rises into the sky like a balloon. This is one example (the submarine is another) of the practical effect of Archimedes' Principle. However, unlike a balloon, which has no propelling or steering system, the airship is dirigible – i.e. it can be guided.

Three types of airship have been constructed in the past – the non-rigid (or blimp), the semi-rigid, and the rigid.

The non-rigid (like Santos-Dumont's airships and the U.S. Navy blimps of the Second World War) consists of a single streamlined gas-tight envelope, with control car, crew quarters and engines slung underneath, and stabilizing fins and control surfaces (rudder to go left or right, elevators to go up or down) attached to the tail.

The semi-rigid (like Nobile's *Norge* and *Italia*) resembles the non-rigid, but has a supporting keel running from nose to tail along the bottom of the envelope.

Both the non-rigid and the semi-rigid are also called pressure airships because they depend on the pressure of the gas and the air ballonets inside the envelope to keep their shape. In this respect they differ completely from the rigid airship.

The rigid airship of 1900–40 kept its shape by means of a rigid metal framework independent of internal gas pressure. This metal framework, a skeleton of aluminium rings and struts, had a fabric cover on the outside and a series of self-contained gas cells suspended from stem to stern inside. In the early Zeppelins the control cars, engine cars, and crew and passenger accommodation were suspended below the hull. In later rigids like the *R100* and *Hindenburg* they were built inside the lower part of the hull itself.

Flying an airship depends to a large extent on constantly adjusting the buoyancy of the craft. A ship can be what is called 'light' or 'heavy' or 'in equilibrium'. This depends on the temperature of the gas in the envelope and the air outside (which in turn depend on the weather, time of day, etc.), the weight of the load, the amount of fuel consumed, altitude, atmospheric pressure and various factors like the weight of snow and rain that may have been picked up. If the ship is 'heavy' the airship pilot may have to release ballast to lighten the load aerostatically, or obtain aerodynamic lift by flying in a nose-up attitude. If the ship is too 'light' he may have to release gas, or take on sea or rain water ballast, or fly in a nose-down attitude.

In normal flight, when the ship is more or less in equilibrium, altitude is controlled by the elevators (operated by an elevator wheel in the control car) in the same way as direction is controlled by the rudder. Take-off and landing can employ aerodynamic or aerostatic techniques, i.e. relying on buoyancy, or engines and elevators, or a bit of both – in either case a large handling crew is needed on the ground to steady the ship or pull it down, likewise a mooring mast by means of which the ship can be docked and undocked.